Natalie & Nat King
Cole

by

Skip Press

CRESTWOOD HOUSE
Parsippany, New Jersey

Library of Congress Cataloging-in-Publication Data
Press, Skip, 1950–
   Natalie & Nat King Cole / by Skip Press. — 1st ed.
     p. cm. — (Star families)
   Includes index.
   ISBN 0-89686-879-6   pbk 0-382-24942-9
   1. Cole, Natalie, 1950– —Juvenile literature. 2. Cole, Nat King, 1917–1965 —Juvenile literature.
 [1. Cole, Natalie, 1950– . 2. Cole, Nat King, 1917-1965. 3. Singers. 4. Afro-Americans—Biography.] I. Title. II. Title:
Natalie and Nat King Cole. III. Series.
ML3930.C53P7 1995
782.42164' 092'2—dc20
[B]   94-22429

Summary: A joint biography of current pop superstar Natalie Cole and her legendary singer/musician
father, Nat King Cole.

Photo Credits
All photos courtesy of AP—Wide World Photos.

Acknowledgments
The author would like to thank the following people for their contribution in compiling this book: Alan Carter, Michael Frank,
Leslie Gourse, Lisa Jefferson, Sujata Murphy, and Wayne Knight of Star Line Records.

Published by Crestwood House, an imprint of Silver Burdett Press.
A Simon & Schuster Company
299 Jefferson Road, Parsippany, NJ 07054

Produced by Great Flying Fish/Spicer, MN

Printed in the United States of America

10 9 8 7 6 5 4 3 2 1

Contents

Looking Back for the Future

Natalie Maria Cole, daughter of legendary singer and musician Nat "King" Cole, was at a crossroads in 1991. Her career had produced a string of hit records, her own television variety show, and adoring fans worldwide. A well-publicized problem with drug abuse during the early 1980s had been behind her for years. But now, in the early 1990s, Natalie felt it was time to reassess her musical career. The surprising direction she took shocked the music industry.

After her professional debut with her father, at age 11, Natalie had never looked back. In 1975, Natalie's first album, *Inseparable*, achieved **gold** status and produced the **Top 10** hit "This Will Be." She won her first two **Grammy Awards** from the National Academy of Recording Arts and Sciences for the album. The success of the recordings that followed made it seem Natalie couldn't miss. Her second album, *Natalie*, went gold in 1976, *Unpredictable* in 1977 went **platinum**, and *Thankful* went platinum the same year. *Natalie . . . Live!* was a gold album in 1978, as was *I Love You So* in 1979. Her singles "Sophisticated Lady," "Mr. Melody," and "Party Lights" were hits, while "I've Got Love on My Mind" was a **Top 5** smash and "Our Love" was a million-seller.

Then came the personal problems, and a long break in recording. In 1987, Natalie overcame her troubles and bounced back with her album *Everlasting*. The record contained the top singles "Pink Cadillac" and "I Live for Your Love" and won her a Grammy nomination, an **Image Award** from the National Association for the Advancement of Colored People (NAACP), and a

Natalie Cole has overcome many personal struggles in order to become the superstar she is today.

Natalie won two NAACP Image Awards in 1992.

Soul Train Best Single (Female) Award. Natalie's 1989 album *Good to Be Back* produced even more hits: "Miss You Like Crazy" and "Wild Women Do," with the latter song featured on the soundtrack of the hit film *Pretty Woman*. This album gave Natalie a Grammy nomination for Best Female Rhythm and Blues Vocal Performance.

But all the success wasn't enough. In her own words, Natalie missed her daddy, and her daddy's music. When she signed with Elektra Entertainment in 1991, the new musical direction she chose was very different from anything she had done before. She decided to record an album of Nat King Cole's hits and to sing his most enduring hit *with* him, through the magic of modern recording techniques. This was a curious undertaking, and people tried to talk her out of it. At that time, the charts were filled with computer-enhanced disco albums. The idea of re-recording the jazzy, "easy listening" songs of Natalie's father surprised most of the music world.

Nat King Cole during his years with Capitol Records

7

Nat King Cole had been a musical genius, recording nearly 700 songs, with hit after hit. From his first chart topper, "Straighten Up and Fly Right," to "Route 66," "Nature Boy," and "Mona Lisa," Cole's distinctive, velvety voice sold millions and millions of records.

The days of Nat's hits were happy ones for the Coles. When Nat King Cole died in 1965, it was a crushing, unexpected blow to teenage Natalie, one that left deep emotional longings in her young mind. Her father had been only in his mid-40s; it seemed to her that life didn't always play fair.

Natalie was greatly influenced by her dad, not only musically but philosophically as well. She knew how he had fought racial predjudice and won, yet been hurt by it. He had given up his popular TV show in 1957 after 64 shows because of the difficulty in attracting national advertisers to a program hosted by a black person. Because he was always a gentleman, his only public explanation for abandoning the show was "Madison Avenue"— the home of the advertising industry—"is afraid of the dark." Natalie grew up watching her father be courteous, yet strong and unswerving in his deeply felt beliefs.

In ignoring critics to pursue her dream of singing with Nat, Natalie was guided by a memory. "I learned a lot from my dad," she commented to a reporter. "And, one thing was always true: he never repeated himself musically . . . . To me, that's what the integrity of an artist is all about."

Amazingly, *Unforgettable With Love*, the album featuring Natalie performing Nat's hits, was a greater success than anything that either of the Coles had ever done alone. The album crossed boundaries of age, race, and culture. The timing of its release was

Natalie won an award for best adult contemporary artist at the American Music Awards in 1992.

perfect—the public was thirsty for nostalgia. In Natalie's words the songs brought back "wonderful memories for other people of songs they heard and loved 30 or 40 years ago." The album sold over 8 million copies and received seven Grammy Awards, including Record of the Year, Album of the Year, Song of the Year, Best Traditional Pop Performance, and Producer of the Year (for David Foster, Natalie, Tommy LiPuma, and André Fischer). It won two **American Music Awards**, and a Public Broadcasting System (PBS) special was made about the project.

The "Unforgettable" single from the album, a duet featuring Natalie singing with her father, reached the Top 10. The accompanying music video was one of the most effective ever made. It blended black-and-white film footage from Nat King Cole's TV show with matching video of present-day Natalie. The video showed just how much of her father's personal charm and warmth Natalie had inherited.

People around the world wanted to hear the songs performed live, so Natalie went on the road, doing concerts continually for almost two years. Then came the difficult question her father had had to ask himself after each hit. Could she do it again?

The Nat King Cole Story

There are conflicting accounts of the actual year of his birth, but it is believed that Nathaniel Adams Coles was born on St. Patrick's Day, March 17, 1919, in Montgomery, Alabama. The family name was Coles. Dropping the *s* came later, in show business. Nat's father, Edward James Coles, Sr., was a Baptist minister. The family moved to Chicago when Nat was four in search of a freer way of life than was possible in the strictly segregated South.

Nat was the youngest child of Edward Coles and his wife, Perlina Adams Coles. His sister Eddie Mae was seven years older than Nat, followed by Edward James, six years older, and Evelyn, four years older. Life was hard for the family, but loving. Perlina led the gospel choir in her husband's new church, played the organ, and taught music to her children.

Nat was a prodigy—a highly talented youngster. When he was four, he taught himself to play "Yes, We Have No Bananas" on the piano and performed the song for his classmates in public school. When he was ten, he won a Thanksgiving musical contest and brought the first prize, a turkey, home to the family.

Nat had a soft, quiet manner. In contrast, his brother Edward (called Eddie by the family) was very outgoing, with a gravelly singing voice. Though his father didn't like it, Eddie played popular music on the upright piano in the living room. Almost every night, Eddie would sneak out of the room he shared with Nat to play clubs on 47th Street, the entertainment center of Chicago. Nat learned music basics from his mother. He learned popular

Nat King Cole played with several different musical groups during the course of his career.

music from Eddie and by listening to songs on the radio. By the time he was a teenager, Nat was sneaking out at night to play music on Chicago's South Side, too.

Nat admired the band leader Duke Ellington. At the age of 16, he was the leader of two groups—a **big band** called the Rogues of Rhythm, and a quintet, Nat Coles and His Royal Dukes. He made little money, playing mostly for meals. The funny thing was, the band members didn't want Nat to sing—they thought he sounded awful! Nat sang in church, but only to please his parents.

Nat idolized piano player Earl "Fatha" Hines. He copied Hines's unique style of playing to develop his own clear, light touch on the keys. Nat played wherever he could. He could often be seen **jamming** with other up-and-coming players who went on to become legends, like guitarist Les Paul and trumpeter Louis Armstrong.

In 1936, Eddie, now a professional musician, came home from a European tour. By then, Nat had decided to follow in his brother's footsteps and pursue a career in music. He was so good that Eddie put together a group with his brother, the Solid Swingers. They played in big clubs and toured the South.

At the Club Panama in south Chicago, Nat fell in love with Nadine Robinson, an attractive dancer who was about ten years older than he. Nadine convinced Nat to go on the road with her in a show called *Shuffle Along*. They got married in Ypsilanti, Michigan, and life looked rosy. But the show failed. The newly-weds ended up broke in Long Beach, California.

They liked the warm, sunny weather of the Los Angeles area, however, and decided to stay. Nat put together a septet, but club owners wanted big bands, not a group of seven. He later told

When Nat's career first began, he was only interested in playing the piano. It was his audience that finally encouraged him to sing.

interviewers that, to make a living, he "played every beer joint from San Diego to Bakersfield." Nadine, meanwhile, worked as a chorus girl and hostess in Los Angeles clubs. To make extra money, Nat wrote songs. After a sermon by his father, he came up with "Straighten Up and Fly Right," which he sold to Mills Music for only $50.

A big break came in 1938, when Nat—who was using the last name Cole by then—put together a trio to play in Bob Lewis's club, the Swanee Inn, on La Brea Avenue in Hollywood. The trio was called "Nat Cole and his Swingsters." The group didn't use a drummer because there was no room on the small stage! With guitarist Oscar Moore and bass player Wesley Prince, the trio got a six-month contract. Nat was only interested in playing piano, but customers kept requesting that he sing. When Nat sang "Sweet Lorraine," the applause was deafening, so he sang even more.

Club owner Bob Lewis was so happy with Nat's singing that one night he placed a toy crown on Nat's head and called him Nat "King" Cole, after the nursery rhyme character "Old King Cole." The name stuck and the trio became known as the "King Cole Trio."

The ever-more-popular group began touring and recording. By 1941, the trio was back in Los Angeles. Bob Lewis booked the group into the Radio Room, on Vine Street in Hollywood, across from NBC Studios. They had received a glowing review in **Down Beat magazine** and had gathered quite a following. They became the **house band** at the 331 Club, which was *the* place to go in those days. Movie stars such as Judy Garland and Lena Horne would sometimes join Nat's trio for a song.

World War II was on, and Wesley Prince was drafted into the army. Johnny Miller became the permanent new bassist and also sang harmony. Nat had flat feet, making him ineligible for the service. Oscar Moore served in the military only briefly.

Although the group had done some recordings and had had a small hit with the song "Vom Vim Veedle," the trio knew they could do better. They did, once the well-known manager Carlos Gastel began handling the group's affairs in 1943. Gastel got them an exclusive seven-year contract with Capitol Records, a brand new company at the time. Capitol bought all the trio's old recordings and made new ones. Ironically, the trio's first big record was "Straighten Up and Fly Right." By May 1944, it had sold 500,000 copies—a major hit.

The legend of Nat King Cole, singer, had begun to form. Although Nat's piano playing would later influence **jazz** legends like Ahmad Jamal, Miles Davis, Bill Evans, and Oscar Peterson, he eventually split from the trio to concentrate on singing. He stayed with the same manager and record company, however, for the rest of his life. With hits like "Nature Boy," "Route 66," "The Christmas Song," "Mona Lisa," "Ramblin' Rose," and, of course, "Unforgettable," Nat King Cole became one of the most beloved singers of all time. By the time of his death, he had sold over nine million albums and made over $50 million for Capitol Records.

The person who perhaps most inspired him to reach such heights, however, did not come into his life until 1946. Her name was Maria Hawkins Ellington, and she would soon become his second wife.

Nat King Cole and Family

In the short years of his life, Nat King Cole created an amazing legacy. He earned so much money for his label, Capitol Records, that the Capitol building in Hollywood was often called the House That Nat King Cole Built. The man cast a very big shadow for any performer following him.

Along with being one of the most popular singers of all time, Nat was a highly creative jazz pianist. His King Cole Trio began at a time when the big band sound was popular, and had a rough time at first. Before long, though, the trio popularized small jazz groups with soft sounds. Featuring a pianist, guitarist, and upright bass player, with no drums (though they later added a bongo player), they were the number one poll winner in their category in the *Metronome* **magazine** poll of 1946. To win *Metronome's* annual readers' survey and be recognized as the best group was quite an honor. Nat was voted best pianist. The trio appeared in short and feature films, and on popular radio shows. They were the best small group in the popular music business.

When Nat King Cole met Maria Hawkins Ellington at New York City's Club Zanzibar in 1946, he was already a star. He was also still married to his first wife, Nadine. Maria had been raised at her aunt's finishing school for young black women in North Carolina. She was sophisticated, beautiful, and getting ahead in show business. She had already sung with three of the biggest bands—Benny Carter, Duke Ellington, and Fletcher Henderson.

But she was still impressed by Nat King Cole.

Nat's first marriage was already in trouble, in part because of career demands. By 1946, he had big hits with "Route 66" and "The Christmas Song." "I Love You for Sentimental Reasons" had been the most popular song in the country, and his group was starring in the *Wildroot Cream Oil Show* on radio. Nat was always busy.

It soon became obvious to Nadine that Nat was in love with Maria and wanted to marry her. Surprisingly, Nadine was understanding and granted Nat a divorce.

Maria and Nat were married on March 28, 1948, at the Abyssinian Baptist Church in Harlem, New York. Maria had an immediate impact on Nat's career. She encouraged him to dress more fashionably and pointed out that he was the *star*, not simply

Nat King Cole married singer Maria Hawkins Ellington in 1948 in Harlem.

Maria's influences were evident in Nat's appearance.

a member of the trio. Maria urged Nat to do more singing and less piano playing. Some people close to Nat thought Maria was "pushy." Whatever her critics thought, today it seems Maria simply wanted the best career possible for her husband.

Jazz listeners—Nat's main fans—were a limited audience. Maria and Nat agreed that pop music was where the money was. Nat Cole had learned that lesson when he began to focus more on singing and less on playing piano.

There was a big reason Nat wanted to make more money. He and Maria became parents shortly after they married. Maria's sister, Carol, died, and Carol's husband died shortly after, leaving their little girl, Carol Claudia, an orphan. Nat and Maria quickly adopted the child, who had been born on October 17, 1944. They called her Cookie.

Seven-pound, 11-ounce Natalie was born on February 6, 1950, in Santa Monica, California. She arrived shortly after the release of Nat's all-time biggest solo hit, "Mona Lisa." Instead of singing that song to Natalie or Cookie, though, he often sang "Ke Mo Ky Mo," from his 1949 album *Nat Cole for Kids*. Her father singing that song at home is one of Natalie's fondest memories.

In later years, the Coles added to their family. They adopted a son, Nat Kelly (called Kelly for short), in 1958, and Maria gave birth to identical twin girls, Casey and Timolin, in 1961.

But it was Natalie's arrival that made Nat a natural father for the first time. Deeply moved by Natalie's birth, Nat told *Ebony* magazine: "I looked at that kid for a long time. I felt something impossible for me to explain in words . . . . Then it came to me. I was a father."

At first, Nat and Maria called the baby Stephanie Maria, then finally Natalie Maria. Nat rarely used her given name, calling her Sweetie instead. The family nickname has endured throughout Natalie's life.

The Coles told *Ebony* shortly after Sweetie was born that their first wish was that she *not* follow in their footsteps. "We hope she won't go into show business," they said. "It just takes too much out of a human being."

The Cole family poses by the pool at their Hollywood home in 1957. From left to right: Maria, Carol (Cookie), Nat, and Natalie (Sweetie).

The Coles lived in Hancock Park, a wealthy area in Los Angeles, when Natalie was born. They were the only black family in the neighborhood. When the Coles moved into their luxurious Tudor-style home shortly before Natalie's birth, the event created a big stir. In typically smooth Nat King Cole style, the family weathered all attacks based on their race.

As little Natalie grew up, she never suspected there had been any problems about living in Hancock Park. As far as she knew, she would live like a show business princess forever. It seemed perfectly normal for her father to pay $2,000 for her and Cookie's first recording session. Her mother was a singer, recording **duets** with her father, and Uncle Eddie, Nat's brother, was a successful musician. Wasn't life supposed to be musical and perfect?

Nat King Cole was escorted to and from performances by security guards after receiving racial threats.

Nat gave this performance in 1956 surrounded by police officers who were
there to protect him from racial attacks.

Nat took Natalie and Cookie everywhere, for rides in his car,
to the recording studio, to visit musician friends. In 1953, when
visiting some friends, Nat told Natalie to "show them how you can
sing." She belted out a rendition of Nat's hit "Walking My Baby
Back Home." Nat's friends were amazed by Natalie's talent—at
age three!

When Nat was on the road doing concerts—which was often—the girls stayed safe at home with their mother. An exception
was a 1959 tour of Latin America. In Mexico, Natalie saw poor
people on the streets. The experience gave her a shock about the
real world. Nat and Maria did not allow their daughters to see poor
areas in the United States until many years later.

Maria and Nat enjoy some local musicians in Argentina during their tour of
Latin America in 1959.

Nat sometimes took the girls on excursions that seemed magical. He flew Cookie and Natalie to New York to see Broadway musicals like *Peter Pan* with Mary Martin. In Syracuse, New York, Natalie saw snow for the first time.

Nat enjoyed spending time with all of his children, but with Natalie, he shared an especially close relationship. On occasion, Natalie sang at the piano with her father. Those were her most treasured times. Sometimes she would stay awake at night, listening for him to go for a late-night snack, then sneak into the kitchen to chat with him alone. When Maria bought Nat a Jaguar convertible for his birthday, he took Natalie for a long ride. She said she felt like his buddy, and thought, "Man, this guy is cool."

Life looked wonderful until October 1964, when Nat became very ill, seemingly overnight. He was thin, pale, and barely able to finish filming his part in the movie *Cat Ballou*. Years of chain-smoking cigarettes had caught up with him, the doctors told Maria.

On January 25, 1965, doctors removed Nat's left lung, but it was too late—cancer had spread throughout his body. He died early in the morning of February 15. Natalie was only 15.

It is never easy being raised in the shadow of a famous parent. But there was a different shadow over young Natalie's life now. It would take her many years to overcome her father's death. The King was gone, and somehow the princess had to survive.

Natalie's Career Is Formed

Natalie's mother, Maria, may have been as influential in the young girl's life as her father. This is not surprising, considering both Maria's influence on Nat and her own love of music. "Every evening my mother would sit in the library and listen to scads of records," Natalie told a reporter in 1993.

Natalie's love for music was influenced by both of her parents.

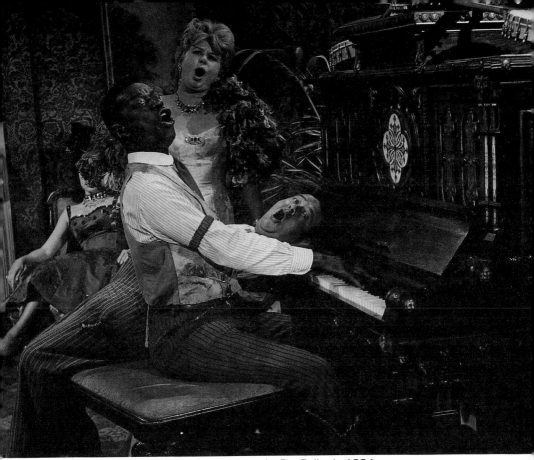

Nat made a rare screen appearance in *Cat Ballou* in 1964.

Moreover, music people were always around the house, particularly at the Coles' annual Fourth of July party. Natalie was impressed by the music of family friends she met there: Harry Belafonte, Nancy Wilson, Ella Fitzgerald, and others. And some music not to the liking of her parents also got Natalie's attention. First there was Elvis Presley, whose success had influenced Nat to record the funny "Mr. Cole Won't Rock and Roll." Then, in the early 1960s, Natalie discovered a new group whose music was sweeping the nation. The group was called the Beatles, and Natalie liked them instantly.

27

Natalie in 1975

The first full song Natalie remembers singing for her father was "Undecided," an Ella Fitzgerald hit. She sang on a Christmas record at age six. Then she and Carol sang with Nat on his recording of "Ain't She Sweet" when Natalie was seven.

In 1961 Natalie made her professional debut. She appeared in her father's "I'm With You" musical revue at the Greek Theatre in Los Angeles, singing "It's a Bore," a song Louis Jordan had sung in the movie *Gigi*. For the performance she received her first paycheck, for $600.

Natalie did not immediately turn professional, however. Maria sent her to boarding school on the East Coast, to make sure her daughter got a fine education. When Nat died, Natalie came back to Los Angeles to be with her family, and began singing **rhythm and blues** in a group. Her group wanted to travel to Hawaii; Natalie would have to drop out of school to go with them. Convinced that her daughter should finish school, Maria told Natalie she would be disowned if she went to Hawaii. Sad and frightened, Natalie stayed behind, graduated from high school, then enrolled at the University of Massachusetts at Amherst.

Though her father's name had opened many doors for her, Natalie's greatest challenge was making a name for herself.

29

Natalie kept singing, but she also wanted to be a doctor, to find a cure for cancer. After all, the disease had killed her father. Her nonmusical ambitions didn't last, though. Natalie sang **Top 40** popular songs with bands, and played in clubs and hotels. Once, on the East Coast, she found herself billed as "Nat King Cole's Daughter." She didn't like that, and said so. Still, she was beginning to get an idea of the size of the musical footsteps she was following.

Natalie is pictured here with Smokey Robinson on the set of her TV show, *Big Break*.

When she turned 21, Natalie inherited $20,000 from her father's estate. She went through the money "like water," she said, spending it all on cars and clothes. Despite being broke, though, she never got financial assistance from anyone. Instead, she supported herself with her music. Shying away from her musical heritage, Natalie sang rock and roll until she began listening to soul singer Aretha Franklin. Not long after that, she started singing **soul** music. She soon signed with an influential agent and got a contract with—who else?—her father's label, Capitol Records.

When her first album, *Inseparable*, came out in 1975, it was an immediate success. It started a run of top-selling albums. Her personal life bloomed at the same time. The Reverend Marvin Yancy and his partner Chuck Jackson were trying to get songs they had written to Aretha Franklin. They couldn't get through to Franklin, but they connected with Natalie. She recorded their songs and let them produce her music, too.

Natalie must have liked working with Marvin Yancy. In 1976 they were married at Chicago's Fountain of Life Church, where Yancy was a minister. The next year their son, Robbie, was born. Like his mother and his grandfather, Robbie was a prodigy. By age three, he was playing drums.

As she became a musical superstar, with gold and platinum albums like *Natalie* (1976) and *Unpredictable* and *Thankful* (both 1977), Nat King Cole's daughter also tried to be a successful wife and mother. But making hit records meant doing numerous shows for her many fans. By the end of the 1970s, Natalie was troubled. There were just too many demands on her. Worn down by the pressures of her schedule and career, she began using drugs.

Natalie first used drugs in college. She experimented with marijuana, ignoring the warnings of long-time family employee "Sparky" Tavares, who told Natalie she would hurt her family and herself by using drugs. She later took drugs to help get her through a demanding performance schedule, not realizing how the drugs were affecting her mental stability.

If her concerts didn't sell out completely, she worried that she was doing something wrong. Her rapid rise to the top made her feel insecure, wondering if she deserved her success. Fights with her record company about what songs she would do, and how the company marketed her records were often bitter. Even throughout these difficult times, Natalie was winning awards, such as her rhythm and blues Grammy for "Sophisticated Lady" in 1976.

Everything suffered, including her marriage. Natalie was facing some difficult problems, and about to learn some big lessons—the hard way.

Getting Beyond the Troubles

Explaining how she almost wrecked her career, Natalie told *Essence* magazine in October 1983 that she let the strain get to her. She became, she said, "a tired lady."

Unfortunately, Natalie was often alone during her ordeal. Her husband, Marvin, wrote her material but did not always go with her on the road. He had his church in Chicago to attend to, as well as his own musical interests.

Natalie is all smiles at the Grammy Awards ceremony in 1989.

Natalie was drawn to the Baptist religion when she met Marvin. She even left her mother's Episcopalian faith to be baptized in Chicago's Third Baptist Church. Her faith was not strong enough, however, to overcome the strains of regular separations from her husband. Their marriage ended in divorce. Natalie tried to escape her emotional pain by using cocaine heavily. But it only made things worse. She would stay at home, crying for hours sometimes, upset by things as minor as a ringing telephone.

During the low times in her life, Natalie was lifted by the memory of her father's struggles against a racist society. She felt her personal problems seemed minor by comparison.

She managed to keep her career going, but just barely. By the early 1980s, she was on her last legs. Her voice was heavily strained from over-use. She had surgery, to remove throat polyps (growths). As she recovered, she realized the mess her life was in. Natalie called her mother for help, asking Maria to take care of young Robbie and her house in Beverly Hills. Natalie had moved there after the breakup of her marriage.

Natalie didn't cure her problems overnight. It took several attempts at rehabilitation, but she finally succeeded. She was able to kick her drug habit. Her music didn't immediately soar to the top of the charts, though, after the singer got her life together. Natalie's personal troubles had been fairly well publicized, and it took time to win her fans back and to polish her tarnished image.

One thing that helped Natalie through the hard times was the memory of her father's struggles. Among his many accomplishments, Nat King Cole had broken the color line in Las Vegas. A big draw to the public, Nat refused to play the Sands Hotel unless the owner treated black patrons the way white patrons were treated. That encouraged other owners to do the same, long before segregation was ended in places like night clubs. For Natalie, overcoming personal problems seemed easy, compared to helping change an entire society.

With a revived career came a new record label, Elektra. Natalie's debut album for the company, *Everlasting*, sold more than one million records. A single from it, "Pink Cadillac," was a big hit. Another very successful song which stood out on the album was one her father had popularized, "When I Fall in Love."

In 1989, Natalie came out with the album *Good to Be Back*, and had a Top 10 single called "Miss You Like Crazy." She hosted her own television program, "Big Break," a show featuring young performers trying to break into the entertainment industry. She even helped First Lady Nancy Reagan promote the "Just Say No" anti-drug campaign.

Natalie added a family member to her group in 1989. Eddie Cole, a talented saxophone player and songwriter who was Natalie's cousin, became her musical director. Onstage, their musical and emotional harmony seemed magical, making Natalie's shows better than ever.

And that wasn't all. She fell in love, with record producer André Fischer. They were married in 1989 at Bethany Baptist Church in Los Angeles and settled in Beverly Hills. Natalie became a stepmother to Fischer's children—Kelly, Liz, and Kyle.

Natalie was not only back, she was back on top. But that didn't mean she was satisfied!

In talks with her manager, Dan Cleary, Natalie revealed a growing desire. While rebuilding her career, she had begun performing Nat King Cole hits. "Nature Boy" and "Ramblin' Rose" often popped up, and she sang a duet of "Unforgettable" with her father's recording of the song. Now she wanted to do 22 of Nat's songs, on a whole new album.

Natalie had weathered too many of life's storms to be deterred from pursuing this dream. She ignored the skeptics and in 1991 came out with *Unforgettable With Love*.

"It had, I guess, a touch of magic," she told the writer Michael Frank in 1993. "I heard from lots of people who had lost their fathers and their mothers. They thought this was a wonderful tribute for a child to pay a parent."

Natalie is pictured here at an autograph signing at a record store in 1992.

By 1993 the album had sold over 8 million copies. Among other things, it bought Natalie and her family a spacious new home in Tarzana, a Los Angeles suburb. Over the piano in the family room, Natalie hung a giant photograph of Nat at a Hammond B-3 organ. The picture had been taken at Capitol Records in 1959.

With the miracle of modern technology, Natalie had recorded an album with her dad, yet managed to make it all her own. It was the most successful album either of them had ever produced. After its release, she spent the next two years on the road, singing for fans across the world.

When Natalie came home from the tour, she faced a new challenge. "Now what?" she wondered.

Taking a Look

The answer to the question was: More of the same, sort of. "I wanted to stick with the ambiance and atmosphere of *Unforgettable With Love*," Natalie said, "but not just make an album that would be a total repetition of what I did before." She called her second album for Elektra *Take a Look*. She went through 40 songs that were popular during her father's era to select the final 18.

Natalie poses with three of the Grammys she won for her high-tech duet with her late father, Nat King Cole.

Not that she had a lot of time to pick new songs. In 1992, she was on the road until 12 days before Christmas. When she wasn't touring or spending time with her family, she was working with charities. Natalie was the 1992 **NARAS MusiCares** Person of the Year. She devoted time and energy to the Children's Diabetes Foundation, the Rainforests Foundation, Save the Heart Foundation, the American Red Cross, AIDS Project L.A., the Minority AIDS Project, and the entertainment industry's Permanent Charities Committee.

Still, the songs on *Take a Look* were not that unfamiliar to Natalie. She had been acquainted with 90 percent of the songs on the album since the time she was ten or eleven.

In July 1993, Natalie opened a three-night stand at the Hollywood Bowl. Before singing the selections from the new album, accompanied by the house orchestra, Natalie told the audience that she had come to see her father play there when she was a child. Later in the show, she wowed the crowd with a duet of "Unforgettable," sung to a film backdrop of her father doing the song. A reviewer for the *Los Angeles Times* told his readers that Natalie's performance of the songs was even better than those from *Unforgettable with Lov*e.

Earlier that year, Natalie had made her TV dramatic acting debut, in the season finale of the NBC series *I'll Fly Away* (the show later moved to PBS). A month later, in March, Natalie performed for millions when she sang at the 1993 Academy Awards.

And so the saga of the amazing, musical Coles continues. Who knows if it will ever end? Natalie's teenage son, Robert Yancy, is

Maria Cole poses by a poster commemmorating the Lifetime Achievement
Award given to her late husband in 1990 by the National Academy of
Recording Arts and Sciences.

now a fine drummer. Will he follow in his grandfather's footsteps, form a popular trio, then put aside his instrument to sing for the audience?

It is doubtful that Natalie Maria "Sweetie" Cole will ever fall from the top again. One reason is her happy family life. She has few worries about her career, or about where things might go from here. She's a loving, devoted mom. She's never shied away from discussing the dangers of drugs with Robbie, Kelly, Liz, and Kyle. Natalie tells it like it is. After all, she's been there, and survived. She doesn't want her kids to make the same mistakes she did.

When Natalie is on the road, she takes her Bible along, and pictures of her family, instead of drugs. Her mother, brother, and sisters are alive and well, and she is happy.

"I will never get to that point again," she told *Redbook* magazine when asked about her drug problem in October 1993. "I know what my foundation is. It helps that I'm a mom. I'm sure my kids look at me onstage, and it must be odd to them. They think, this can't be the same person who tells me to pick up my clothes all the time."

Sometimes, when we think about how the world has changed since Nat King Cole began his career, we can't help but be amazed. There is little danger that Natalie Cole will be physically attacked by racists, as her father was at a show in Birmingham, Alabama. Nowadays, when people around the world listen to Nat and Natalie, singing alone or together, it is the music that matters, and nothing else.

In January 1994, Natalie Cole opened the festivities at the Super Bowl by singing "The Star-Spangled Banner." She had never looked more beautiful, or happy. In February, she traveled

Natalie belts out "The Star-Spangled Banner" during opening ceremonies of Super Bowl XXVIII.

to Sun City, South Africa, for a five-day engagement, becoming the first African American to perform in her own show in that formerly heavily segregated country. If you could have been there, watching the faces in the audience light up as Natalie began to sing, you might have imagined another presence on the stage. Somewhere near Natalie Maria "Sweetie" Cole—and not far from the piano, no doubt—wearing his customary fedora hat and a broad smile, hovered the spirit of Nat King Cole, humming along happily.

Perhaps there's just one word to describe such an amazing experience. And that word could only be . . .

Unforgettable.

Glossary

American Music Awards Awards given annually in a nationally televised show to musical artists in the following categories: pop/rock, soul/rhythm and blues, country, heavy metal/hard rock, rap/hip-hop, and adult contemporary. Winners are artists with the highest number of record sales.

big band A jazz or dance band the size of an orchestra.

***Down Beat* magazine** A popular magazine about musical artists and the music business.

duet A song that two people perform together.

gold Signifies sales of at least 500,000 record albums or compact discs (CDs).

Grammy Awards Awards given annually by the National Academy of Recording Arts and Sciences to the best artist or song in various categories, as voted by the academy's members. "Grammy" is short for gramophone, an early form of record player.

house band A band that is hired to perform at a club on a regular basis, as the main act or as background for other performers.

Image Award A yearly award given by the National Association for the Advancement of Colored People (NAACP) to those who help promote a good image for African American people.

jamming Improvising (making up) music on the spot with other musicians.

jazz Lively music that originated in New Orleans, Louisiana, at the beginning of the twentieth century. It is characterized by intricate rhythms and freedom of melody.

***Metronome* magazine** A magazine for and about the recording business. It was the most influential magazine for musicians when the Nat King Cole Trio was starting out.

NARAS MusiCares An organization within the National Academy of Recording Arts and Sciences devoted to helping worthy charities.

platinum Signifies sales of at least one million record albums or compact discs (CDs).

rhythm and blues A folk-based form of black music marked by strong, repetitive rhythms and simple melodies.

soul Expressive, passionate black music developed in the 1950s, with roots in gospel (church) music and rhythm and blues.

Soul Train A popular, long-running TV dance program that emphasizes black music.

Star Search A television talent show featuring performers trying to break into the entertainment industry.

Top 5 The 5 most popular songs in the country in a given week, as judged by *Billboard* magazine and other sources.

Top 10 The 10 most popular songs in the country in a given week, as judged by *Billboard* magazine or other sources.

Top 40 The 40 most popular songs in the country in a given week, as judged by various sources. Also, a repertoire of popular songs both past and present, played by bands in music clubs and restaurants.

Index